Why Government Is the Problem

Milton Friedman

Hoover Institution on War, Revolution and Peace
Stanford University
1993

The Hoover Institution on War, Revolution and Peace,
founded at Stanford University in 1919 by Herbert Hoover,
who went on to become the thirty-first president of the United
States, is an interdisciplinary research center for advanced study
on domestic and international affairs. The views expressed in its publications
are entirely those of the authors and do not necessarily reflect the views of
the staff, officers, or Board of Overseers of the Hoover Institution.

www.hoover.org

Hoover Institution Press Publication—
Essays in Public Policy No. 39

First printing, 1993
19 18 17 16 15   20 19 18 17 16 15

Manufactured in the United States of America

Library of Congress Cataloging-in-Publication Data
Friedman, Milton, 1912–2006.
    Why government is the problem / by Milton Friedman.
    p.   cm.— (Essays in public policy; no. 39)
ISBN-10: 0-8179-5442-2 (pbk.: alk. paper)
ISBN-13: 978-0-8179-5442-0 (pbk.: alk. paper)
ISBN-13: 978-0-8179-5443-7 (epub)
ISBN-13: 978-0-8179-5447-5 (mobi)
ISBN-13: 978-0-8179-5448-2 (PDF)
    1. United States—Economic policy—1981–   .
2. United States—Politics and government—1981–1989.
3. United States—Politics and government—1989–1993.
4. Free enterprise—United States
I. Title. II. Series.
HB106.8.F743   1993
338—dc20   93-6673

EXECUTIVE SUMMARY

The major social problems of the United States—deteriorating education, lawlessness and crime, homelessness, the collapse of family values, the crisis in medical care—have been produced by well-intended actions of government. That is easy to document. The difficult task is understanding why government is the problem. The power of special interests arising from the concentrated benefits of most government actions and their dispersed costs is only part of the answer. A more fundamental part is the difference between the self-interest of individuals when they are engaged in the private sector and the self-interest of the same individuals when they are engaged in the government sector. The result is a government system that is no longer controlled by "we, the people." Instead of Lincoln's government "of the people, by the people, and for the people," we now have a government "of the people, by the bureaucrats, for the bureaucrats," including the elected representatives who have become bureaucrats. At the moment, term limits appear to be the reform that promises to be most effective in curbing Leviathan.

WHY GOVERNMENT
IS THE PROBLEM

When a preacher gives a sermon, he usually has a text. Generally, the text expresses a thought that he agrees with and is going to expound. I have been trying to find the word for an antitext because I have a text for this essay that I am persuaded is wholly wrong. The text comes from the September—October 1991 issue of *Freedom Review*, about as inappropriate a place as possible. It is the statement, "Reagan's fatuous doctrine that government is the problem."[1] That's my text—or my antitext—for this essay.

The text leaves me two tasks: one easy, one difficult. The first task is to demonstrate that government is the problem; that's the easy task. The hard task is to understand why government is the problem. Why is it that able, public-spirited people produce such different results according to whether they operate in the political or the economic market? Why is it that if a random sample of the people who read this essay and are not at present in Washington were to replace those who are in Washington, our policies would very likely not be improved? That is the real puzzle for me.

As to the easy task, let me just first count the ways—to plagiarize words from a love poem—in which government is the problem. Let's list our major social problems and ask where they come from.

Adapted from the 1991 Wriston Lecture, presented in New York City on November 19, 1991, under the auspices of the Manhattan Institute.Richard Stern, and Stephen Stigler.

Showing That Government Is Their Problem

Education

One major social problem is clearly the deterioration of our educational system. Next to the military, education is the largest socialist industry in the United States. Total government spending on schooling—I call it schooling rather than education because not all schooling is education and vice versa—comes close to total government spending on defense, if, with the so-called peace dividend, it is not already greater. The amount spent per pupil in the past thirty years has tripled in real terms after allowing for inflation. Although input has tripled, output has been going down. Schools have been deteriorating. That problem is unquestionably produced by government.

Lawlessness and Crime

If there is any function of government that all but the most extreme anarchist libertarians will agree is appropriate, it is to protect individuals in society from being coerced by other individuals, to keep you from being hit over the head by a random or nonrandom stranger. Is there anybody who will say we are performing that function well? Far from it. Why not? In part because there are so many laws to break; and the more laws there are to break, the harder it is to prevent them from being broken, not only because law enforcement means are inadequate but, even more, because a larger and larger fraction of the laws fail to command the allegiance of the people. You can rigidly enforce only those laws that most people believe to be good laws, that is, laws that proscribe actions that they would avoid even in the absence of laws. When laws render illegal actions that many or most people regard as moral and proper, they can be enforced only by brute force. Speed laws are an obvious example; alcohol prohibition, a more dramatic one.

I believe a major source of our current lawlessness, in particular the destruction of the inner cities, is the attempt to prohibit so-called drugs. I say so-called because the most harmful drugs in the

United States are legal: cigarettes and alcohol. We once tried to prohibit the consumption of alcohol at tremendous cost. We are now trying to prohibit the use of narcotics at tremendous cost. The particular consequence that I find most indefensible is the havoc wreaked on residents of Colombia, Peru, and other countries because we cannot enforce our own laws. I have yet to hear an acceptable justification of that consequence. Coming back home, whether or not you believe that it is an appropriate function of government to prevent people from voluntarily ingesting items that you regard as harmful to them—and whether you believe that it is an appropriate function of government because of the harm to them or to third parties—the attempt to do so has been a failure. It has caused vastly more harm to innocent victims, including the public at large and especially the residents of the inner cities, than any good it has done for those who would choose to use the prohibited narcotics if they were legal. There would be some innocent victims (e.g., crack babies) even if drugs were legalized. But they would be far fewer, and much more could be done to reduce their number and help the remainder.

Homelessness

What produced the current wave of homelessness around the country, which is a disgrace and a scandal? Much of it was produced by government action. Rent control has contributed, though it has been even more damaging in other ways, as has the governmental decision to empty mental facilities and turn people out on the streets and urban renewal and public housing programs, which together have destroyed far more housing units than they have built and let many public housing units become breeding grounds for crime and viciousness.

Family Values

Government alone has not been responsible for the extraordinary collapse that has occurred in family values and the resulting explosion in the number of teenage pregnancies, illegitimate births, and one-parent families. Government has, however, contributed to these social problems in major degree. Charles Murray's study of these phenomena in his book *Losing Ground* provides persuasive evidence that these social problems owe a great deal to mistaken and misdirected governmental policies.[2] Personally, I would add another misdirected governmental policy, which he does not consider, that I believe played a key role in the breakdown of social and cultural values—though by a rather indirect route—namely, military conscription. But that is an argument for a different day.

Housing

Another social problem is the high cost of housing and the destruction of housing. The North Bronx looks like the pictures recently coming from Yugoslavia of areas that have been shelled. There is no doubt what the cause is: rent control in the city of New York, both directly and via the government taking over many dwelling units because rent control prevented owners from keeping them up. The same results have been experienced wherever rent control has been adopted and enforced, though New York is by all odds the worst case.

In addition, the proliferation all over the country of building regulations, zoning laws, and other governmental actions has raised the cost of housing drastically. A friend in California has been a building contractor since before World War II. I asked him, "Suppose you were to build the identical house today that you built in 1945 in one of your large housing projects, and suppose that the price of labor, material, and so on were the same now as it was then. How much more would it cost you now than it did then because you must get government permits and demonstrate that you have satisfied government requirements?" He thought about it a while and finally concluded, "At least one-quarter of the total cost."

Medical Care

Government has played an increasingly large role in medical care. For decades, total spending on medical care was about 3 to 5 percent of national income. It is now 12 or 13 percent and rising. The acceleration of spending dates from the introduction of Medicare and Medicaid in 1965. In an earlier essay of mine (*Input and Output in Medical Care*, Hoover Essays in Public Policy series), I cited figures on hospital cost per patient day, adjusted for inflation. The cost was twenty-six times as high in 1989 as it had been in 1946 ($545 compared with $21); personnel per occupied hospital bed was seven times as high (4.6 compared with 0.7), while the number of hospital beds per 1,000 population had been cut in half (from 10.3 to 4.9). Medical care has advanced greatly since 1946, but it did so before 1965 as well as after, yet most of the increase in cost occurred after 1965. Those seven times as many people per hospital bed are clearly not people who are attending to patients; they are mostly people who are filling in forms to satisfy government requirements.

Financial System

You are all fully aware of the weakness of our financial system. Is there any doubt that that weakness owes much to Washington? The savings and loans crisis was produced by government, first by the accelerating inflation of the 1970s, which destroyed the net worth of many savings and loan institutions, then by poor regulation in the 1980s, by the increase in the amount covered by deposit insurance to $100,000, and, more recently, by the heavy-handed handling of the crisis. You know the litany; I don't have to spell it out.

Highway Congestion

We all complain about highway congestion. That is interesting for a different reason. The private automobile industry is able to produce all the automobiles anybody wants to drive, but the government is apparently not able to produce a comparably adequate highway system, a clear contrast.

Airports

A similar contrast exists with respect to airlines and airports. The private aircraft industry has been able to build all the aircraft that the commercial airlines wanted to buy, and the airlines have been able to recruit the necessary pilots, attendants, mechanics, and so on. Where is the bottleneck? In airports, in air control facilities. Why? Because those are run by the government.

Miscellaneous

I have not even mentioned the botched economic policies: the reverse Reaganomics that the Bush administration practiced contributed to the recession of 1990—1991, condemned us to a very slow and erratic recovery from a mild recession, and, very probably, promises a relatively slow 1990s, almost regardless of what the Clinton administration does. Nor have I mentioned such things as over-regulation of industry or agricultural policies under which taxpayers pay people to grow crops that are going to be destroyed or stored or given away. I have not mentioned tariffs and quotas or affirmative action and wage and hour laws.

In light of this list, is there any doubt that government is the problem?

None of this means that government does not have a very real function. Indeed, the tragedy is that because government is doing so many things it ought not to be doing, it performs the functions it ought to be performing badly. The basic functions of government are to defend the nation against foreign enemies, to prevent coercion of some individuals by others within the country, to provide a means of deciding on our rules, and to adjudicate disputes.[3]

I wonder if any of the liberal pundits who go around saying that the private market and capitalism, not government, is the problem can name any corresponding set of major problems that afflict our society that derive from private enterprise.

Their knee-jerk answer is clear: pollution. Private enterprise, they will say, is responsible for polluting the air, for polluting the water, for destroying the earth. I suggest to them that they compare the pollution in countries that have been run by the government, such as Poland or the Soviet Union or Romania, with the pollution in this country. The difference is not that our government has been more efficient in avoiding pollution; it is that private enterprise finds that it is not profitable to pollute; it is more profitable to avoid pollution. There is a real function for government in respect to pollution: to set conditions and, in particular, define property rights to make sure that the costs are borne by the parties responsible. Actual government policy, however, has been neither efficient nor effective. An example is the recently passed Clean Air Bill. It will clean the pockets of industry far more effectively than it will clean the air.

Explaining Why Government Is The Problem

One common explanation of why government is the problem, and one that I have often stressed, is the influence of special interests. Government actions often provide substantial benefits to a few while imposing small costs on many. A dramatic example occurred to me recently when I was talking to a taxicab driver in New York City. (Taxicab drivers seem to be the source of all anecdotes.) I have long been interested in the problem of regulation of taxicabs, so I asked him the market price of a medallion to drive a taxicab. As you know, the number of taxicabs is limited by government fiat. The medallion signifying permission to operate a taxicab is transferable and traded in a relatively free market. Its current price is apparently now somewhere between $100,000 and $125,000.

If the limitation on the number of taxis were removed, the benefits would greatly exceed the losses. Consumers would benefit by having a wider range of alternatives. The number of cabs would go up and so would the demand for drivers. To attract more drivers, the earnings of drivers would have to rise. In economic jargon, the supply curve of drivers is positively sloped.

Why does the limitation of the number of cabs persist? The answer is obvious: the people who now own those medallions would lose and they know it. Although they are few, they would make a lot of noise at city hall. The people who would end up driving the additional cabs do not know that they would have new jobs or better jobs. There is no New Yorker who would find it worth his or her time and effort to lobby city hall to remove the arbitrary limitation on medallions simply to get better cab service. It does not pay the individual taxi riders to do so. They are right; it is rational ignorance on their part not to do so.

The phenomenon of concentrated benefits and dispersed costs is a valid explanation for many governmental programs. However, I believe it does not go far enough to explain the kind of situation in which we now are. For example, it does not explain why, once a government enterprise is established, it should be so much less efficient than a comparable private enterprise. Maybe concentrated benefits lead to the establishment of a government enterprise. However, why on those grounds should the U.S. Post Office be less efficient than United Parcel Service?

One answer is that the incentive of profit is stronger than the incentive of public service. In one sense I believe that is right, but in another sense I believe it is completely wrong. The people who run our private enterprises have the same incentive as the people who are involved in our government enterprises. In all cases the incentive is the same: to promote their own interest. My old friend Armen Alchian, who is a professor at the University of California at Los Angeles, put the point this way: There is one thing, he said, that you can trust everybody to do and that is to put his interest above yours. The people who run our private enterprises are people of the same kind as those who run our public enterprises, just as the Chinese in Hong Kong are the same as the Chinese in Mainland China; just as the West Germans and the East Germans were not different people, yet the results were vastly different.

The point is that self-interest is served by different actions in the private sphere than in the public sphere. The bottom line is different. An enterprise started by a group of people in the private sphere may succeed or fail. Most new enterprises fail (if the enterprise were clearly destined for success, it would probably already exist). If the enterprise fails, it loses money. The people who own it have a clear bottom line. To keep it going, they have to dig into their own pockets. They are reluctant to do that, so they have a strong incentive either to make the enterprise work or to shut it down.

Suppose the same group of people start the same enterprise in the government sector and the initial results are the same. It is a failure; it does not work. They have a very different bottom line. Nobody likes to admit that he has made a mistake, and they do not have to. They can argue that the enterprise initially failed only because it was not pursued on a large enough scale. More important, they have a much different and deeper pocket to draw on. With the best intentions in the world, they can try to persuade the people who hold the purse strings to finance the enterprise on a larger scale, to dig deeper into the pockets of the taxpayers to keep the enterprise going. That illustrates a general rule: If a private enterprise is a failure, it closes down—unless it can get a government subsidy to keep it going; if a government enterprise fails, it is expanded. I challenge you to find exceptions.

The general rule is that government undertakes an activity that seems desirable at the time. Once the activity begins, whether it proves desirable or not, people in both the government and the private sector acquire a vested interest in it. If the initial reason for undertaking the activity disappears, they have a strong incentive to find another justification for its continued existence.

A clear example in the international sphere is the International Monetary Fund (IMF), which was established to administer a system of fixed exchange rates. Whether that is a good system or a bad system is beside the point. In 1971, after President Nixon closed the gold window, the fixed exchange rate system collapsed and was replaced by a system of floating exchange rates. The IMF's function disappeared, yet, instead of being disbanded, it changed its function and expanded. It became a relief agency for backward countries and proceeded to dig deeper into the pockets of its sponsors to finance its new activities. At Bretton Woods, two agencies were established: one to administer a fixed exchange rate system and the other, the World Bank, to perform the function of promoting development. Now you have two agencies to promote development, both of them, in my opinion, doing far more harm than good.

Let me take a very different example in the United States. At the end of World War II, we had wage and price controls. Under wartime inflationary conditions, many employers found it difficult to recruit employees. To get around the limitations of wage control, many began to offer health care as a fringe benefit to attract workers. As a new benefit, it took some years for the Internal Revenue Service to get around to requiring the cost of the medical care to be included in the reported taxable income of the employees. By the time it did, workers had come to regard nontaxable medical care provided by the employer as a right—or should I say entitlement? They raised such a big political fuss that Congress legislated nontaxable status for employer-provided medical care.

That excuse disappeared once wage and price controls were eliminated, but the tax exemption of health benefits continued. The result was to create a medical system in which it came to be taken for granted that employees would get their health benefits through their employers. In this indirect way, wartime wage control, abolished after the end of the war, was a major factor that produced the current drive for socialized medicine, strongly fostered by a large part of the business community.

Liberal pundits will tell you that the problem is that the public wants the goodies that government supposedly provides but is too stingy to pay for them. If only, liberals say, we could get those greedy, stingy people to provide us with more taxes, we could solve all these problems. They may be partly right, but only partly. For example, that explanation cannot be the reason we have agricultural subsidies. Do the people of this country really want to pay farmers to grow goods and throw them away or give them away at low prices abroad? To say that the public wants the goodies that government supplies may be true for Medicare and Medicaid but surely not for agricultural subsidies or restrictions on the import of Japanese cars, restrictions that raised by perhaps $2,000 or so the cost of a car to a member of the public and, incidentally, did not prevent the decline of the U.S. auto industry. It is not true for sugar import quotas. If you could have a public vote on whether consumers want to pay twice the world price for sugar, do you think that there would be an overwhelming vote saying yes?

On the contrary, when people have the opportunity to vote on those issues, they overwhelmingly vote the other way. The public at large thinks that government is too big. People know they are not getting their money's worth for the taxes they pay. In California, where I live and where propositions can be put on the ballot so that you can have direct democracy, the people voted for Proposition 13, which started the tax revolt. Later, they voted for what was called the Gann Limit on total government spending. Californians voted in 1991 to limit the terms of state legislators and, in 1992, the terms of members of Congress. Connecticut has a graduated income tax today not because the people voted for it but because Weicker is governor. Repeated ballot measures designed to increase graduation of the state income tax had earlier been defeated.

However, the liberal pundits are wrong in a more fundamental way. The problem is not that government is spending too little but that it is spending too much. The problem in schooling is that government is spending too much on the wrong things. The problem in health care is that government is spending too much on the wrong things. The end result has been that government has become a self-generating monstrosity. Abraham Lincoln talked about a government of the people, by the people, for the people. What we now have is a government of the people, by the bureaucrats, including the legislators who have become bureaucrats, for the bureaucrats.

Again, let me emphasize, the problem is not that bureaucrats are bad people. The problem, as the Marxists would say, is with the system, not with the people. The self-interest of people in government leads them to behave in a way that is against the self-interest of the rest of us. You remember Adam Smith's famous law of the invisible hand: People who intend only to seek their own benefit are "led by an invisible hand to serve a public interest which was no part of" their intention. I say that there is a reverse invisible hand: People who intend to serve only the public interest are led by an invisible hand to serve private interests which was no part of their intention.

I believe our present predicament exists because we have gradually developed governmental institutions in which the people effectively have no voice. A recent study by James Payne brought this home to me very clearly. Examining fourteen different government hearings dealing with spending issues, Payne found that "1,014 witnesses appeared in favor of the spending. Only 7 could be classified as opponents. In other words, pro-spending witnesses outnumbered anti-spending witnesses 145 to 1." Striking as that is, an even more important finding was that "of the 1,060 witnesses who appeared, 47 percent were federal administrators, and another 10 percent were state and local officials. An additional 6 percent were congressmen themselves." Thus 63 percent of the witnesses in favor of the spending were from government. They were telling us that they should spend our money, I won't say for their benefit but for what they believed, or said they believed, was our benefit. Payne added, *"Overwhelmingly,*

Congress's views on spending programs are shaped by government officials themselves."[4] What is true of spending proposals is equally true of other governmental measures: sugar quotas, the tax exemption of medical care provided by employers, the agricultural subsidies, and so on down the line.

The problem of concentrated benefits and diffused costs is a real problem. However, I do not believe that at the moment it is the key problem. The key problem is that we are unable to practice what we preach because of what has happened to the governmental structure. We preach free enterprise to the newly freed communist countries. We tell them to privatize, privatize, privatize, while we socialize, socialize, socialize.

What can we do about it? We do not have to punish ourselves. This is a great country; it is the richest country in the world with the highest standard of living. It is an extraordinary tribute to the virtues of the free market that, with less than 50 percent of the country's total resources, the private sector can produce a level of living that is the envy of most of the world.[5] We, the people, must once again rule. It will take a major change in the political structure, I believe, to make that possible.

The one movement that I see on the horizon that offers promise is the movement toward term limits, a move that would debureaucratize at least Congress. Heretical though it may seem, it would be nice to get back to the spoils system instead of the civil service. That would debureaucratize the administration. We now have people in secure, permanent positions whose well-being depends on having government play a major and ever-larger role. Although I see no possibility of getting back to the spoils system, term limits on members of Congress would debureaucratize not only Congress itself but also congressional staffs, about the only governmental employees who are not subject to civil service rules and tenure.

There is widespread public support for term limits. Colorado passed term limits for both state legislators and members of Congress in 1991. California passed term limits for state legislators in 1991 and joined thirteen other states in passing term limits for members of Congress in the 1992 election, so fifteen states now have legislated such limits. The number of votes for term limits in the fourteen states that had the issue on the ballot exceeded the nationwide popular vote for Governor Clinton! This is truly an idea whose time has come. Of course, members of Congress will tell you that it is unconstitutional for individual states to limit their terms. Maybe it is, but it should be tested, and Congress certainly has the power to propose a constitutional amendment to that effect. At any rate, something drastic is needed to reverse the direction in which we are moving.

The United States has a great heritage and a great history. Since the beginning of our republic, every generation has been better schooled than its predecessor and has had a higher standard of living. The coming generation threatens to be the first for which that is not true, and that would be a major tragedy.

Notes

1. E. J. Dionne, "Why Americans Hate Politics," *Freedom Review*, September–October 1991, P. 45.
2. Charles Murray, *Losing Ground: American Social Policy, 1950–1980* (New York: Basic, 1984).
3. As recent books by Huber and Olson amply demonstrate, the government is not performing its function of adjudicating disputes very well. See Peter W. Huber, *Liability: The Legal Revolution and Its Consequences* (New York: Basic, 1988), and *Galileo's Revenge* (New York: Basic, 1991); Walter K. Olson, *The Litigation Explosion* (New York: Dutton, 1991).
4. Quotations from James L. Payne, "Why Congress Can't Kick the Tax and Spend Habit," *Imprimis* (Hillsdale College) 20, no. 5 (May 1991).
5. Government spending at all levels, federal, state, and local, in 1992 was about 43 percent of the national income. In addition, mandated expenditures plus costs imposed by regulations, tariffs, quotas, and so on in effect commandeer a healthy slice of the 57 percent nominally spent by the private sector. I conclude that the private sector controls "less than 50 percent of the country's total resources."

QUESTION-AND-ANSWER SESSION

QUESTION: Why do you believe that this country is not getting the government it wants when the Democrats control practically all the legislative bodies in the country and we have wet liberal Republicans like your esteemed governor in California? The spenders are elected. Reagan seems to have been an aberration.

FRIEDMAN: It has nothing to do with Democrats or Republicans. They are all in the position that I described: they are all seeking to promote their own self-interest. Reagan was a real aberration in the sense that he was the first president in my lifetime who was elected not because he was saying what the people wanted to hear but because the people had come around to wanting to hear what he was saying. He said the same thing in 1980 that he had said in 1964 in supporting Goldwater. He could not have been elected in 1964, and he was elected in 1980. In that sense he was an aberration, but, in the sense of reflecting the real underlying feeling of the population, I do not think he was.

As I say, I believe that the reason that we are not getting the government the people want is because there is no way in which they can make their wants effective. It is the same thing as with the cab business. The people in one district can choose not to reelect their member of Congress, but that will not change the composition of the government as a whole. You have to change the system and make it possible for the people's will to be heard. Take California. How do I know that the people are not getting the legislation they want? I know that because they overwhelmingly passed term limits on legislators and a sharp reduction in permissible expenditures on legislative assistance. When they could vote on the legislature as a whole, they voted very differently than they voted on individual legislators. On your logic, Russia was getting the government its people wanted.

QUESTION: How important were World War II and the War Production Board in convincing the public of the power of government to "do good"? Second, and I'll tie them together, how important was inflation in the seventies for the success of Reagan? Therefore, are ideas not that important?

FRIEDMAN: On the first issue, I believe the Great Depression was the overwhelmingly important event that persuaded the public that government could do good. The United States was able for 150 years or more to maintain a system that was predominantly private, in which total government spending—federal, state, and local—until 1930 was never more than about 10 or 12 percent of national income; federal spending in 1929 was 3 percent of national income. The United States was able to maintain that because the public at large was persuaded that government was the problem and that the private enterprise system was the way to go. I may say they were not persuaded of that by the intellectuals because the intellectuals—at least by the turn of the century—were predominantly socialists.

It is interesting to ask how countries become free. Why was it that the United States did not get involved in these socialist measures much earlier? Accident played a large part. In the 1830s, to go back to the early history of our country, state after state did get involved. The states owned banks—the Bank of Ohio, the Bank of Indiana. The states constructed turnpikes and canals and were engaged in manufacturing businesses. Then came the panic of 1837, and a major depression in which most of these state enterprises went broke, and the public at large became persuaded that the states could not run those things. I believe that is one reason why private enterprise flourished for the next century.

In the 1930s, it went the other way. It is ironic that the Great Depression was produced by government but was blamed on the private enterprise system. The Federal Reserve System explained in its 1933 annual report how much worse things would have been if the Federal Reserve had not behaved so well, yet the Federal Reserve was the chief culprit in making the depression as deep as it was. So the government produced the depression, the private enterprise system got blamed for it, and there was a tremendous change in attitudes. When you say ideas are not important, that change in attitudes would not have been possible if the groundwork had not been laid by the socialist intellectuals in the 1920s. It is interesting to note that every economic plank of the 1928 Socialist party platform has by now been either wholly or partly enacted.

So ideas are important, but they take a long time and are not important in and of themselves. Something else has to come along that provides a fertile ground for those ideas. I mentioned the adoption of floating exchange rates in 1971; it was the same thing. Many economists during the previous twenty years had been talking about how much more desirable floating exchange rates would be, but they never got anywhere until gold started leaving the United States and Nixon closed the gold window because there was nothing else he could do. All of a sudden you had a crisis. What happened then was determined by the ideas that had already been explored and developed.

I do believe that ideas have an influence, although I also believe that the accelerating inflation of the seventies was important in enabling Reagan to be elected. However, the accelerating inflation was even more important in causing our present difficulties because of what it did to the tax system through bracket creep. I once attended a breakfast with Senator Long when he was chairman of the Senate Finance Committee; I remember very well his saying, "You know we never could have adopted by legislation the rates of tax we now impose on low and middle incomes. When those rates were adopted, they were on high-income people, but inflation made them applicable to low-income people." I believe that was an important effect of inflation on expanding government.

QUESTION: I think your work was very influential in convincing a lot of people that the roots of the inflation of the seventies were fighting the Vietnam War, making the Great Society, and doing it by creating money. In the 1980s, it looks as if we financed the cold war and continued the Great Society, but, instead of monetary financing, we did it with debt. How serious do you think the debt overhang is?

FRIEDMAN: I do not believe the debt overhang is the real problem. I believe the real problem is government spending. Government debt is a problem in the long run. Obviously, if the government continues to run deficits for a long period of time, it will sooner or later have to monetize them. So I do not deny that is a real problem. However, it is a mistake to concentrate on the debt as such instead of concentrating on why the debt was created, which is by excessive government spending. What is called a deficit is a form of taxation. It is a very bad form of taxation, but it is a form of taxation. However, it does have some good features. The deficit is the only thing that is keeping spending from going up still faster. Moreover, I do not know of any component of government expenditures that does less harm than the payment of interest. If interest rates tomorrow were zero so that government did not have to pay any interest, what would happen to the money it saved? Do you think it would reduce the deficit? You are kidding yourself.

QUESTION: Can you tell us—I don't happen to know—under what circumstances you first said the famous words "There's no such thing as a free lunch"?

FRIEDMAN: Peggy Noonan, who has written some very good words that you have all heard such as "Read my lips"—it's too bad she wasn't able to enforce the words she wrote—asked me if I could remember when I first used the words "There's no such thing as a free lunch." The answer is no, I don't remember. However, I am not really the originator of that statement. A colleague of mine at the Hoover Institution traced it back to some time in the nineteenth century in the parlance of saloons: If you bought a beer, they would give you a free lunch. That's where the phrase originally came from. It was made popular by Robert Heinlein, a science fiction writer who wrote a wonderful novel called *The Moon Is a Harsh Mistress*. The novel's setting is a settlement on the moon that revolts using the motto TAN STAAFL (There ain't no such thing as a free lunch). I may say that the revolution was a success because of a wonderful near-human computer.

QUESTION: I hope you will not think this question a digression; I would submit that it is central to the debate. If there is one thing that distinguishes our society as an economy from all others, it is the diversity of our population. I would like to know specifically what steps you would recommend to turn the diversity of our population into a competitive advantage in the global economy.

FRIEDMAN: I do not believe in the concept of a competitive advantage in the global economy. We are not harmed by other people improving their standard of living relative to ours; we are helped. The notion of competitiveness, of which so much is spoken, makes sense for an individual enterprise but it does not make any sense for a country. Poor countries can trade with rich countries. A country that is inefficient in almost everything can still trade with one that is very efficient. The economists have a name for that: what determines things is comparative advantage, not absolute advantage. Almost all talk about national competitiveness rests on the fallacy of not considering what determines the exchange rate. It assumes a given exchange rate and then all sorts of things follow that in practice do not occur because, if the exchange rate is inappropriate, it cannot be maintained.

Let me return to your basic and more important question: how can we take advantage of the diversity of our population in order to maintain the well-being of all of us? The answer is straightforward: by reducing the role of government. A book just recently published by the Manhattan Institute is Linda Chavez's excellent *Out of the Barrio*, which gives another example of how government creates problems, in this case, through bilingualism. She discusses that very effectively, and I recommend her book to all of you. Bilingualism is another example of the people involved not wanting what is imposed on them. How did the Americans absorb the immigrants in the nineteenth century? How did they absorb my mother and father, who came to this country at the ages of fourteen and sixteen, respectively, with nothing but their hands? I assure you that there was no welfare office they could go to when they came. There was no governmental relief, but they were able to make their way because there were no barriers to their doing so. I talked about taxicabs in New York. One of the most important programs you could have for the disadvantaged in New York would be to eliminate the limitations on cab licenses. Look at the city of Washington, where for a long time there were essentially no limits; the cabdrivers are far more heterogeneous in Washington, D.C., than they are in New York.

The great virtue of a free market system is that it does not care what color people are; it does not care what their religion is; it only cares whether they can produce something you want to buy. It is the most effective system we have discovered to enable people who hate one another to deal with one another and help one another.